... Simple Machines ...

Screw in a spin

TOMSING

Here is Screw
with a new kite.
Screw has built it. The kite
is red and its tail is tied
with purple bows.

Screw is really happy.
It's getting windy
so it's a perfect day to
try out the new kite.

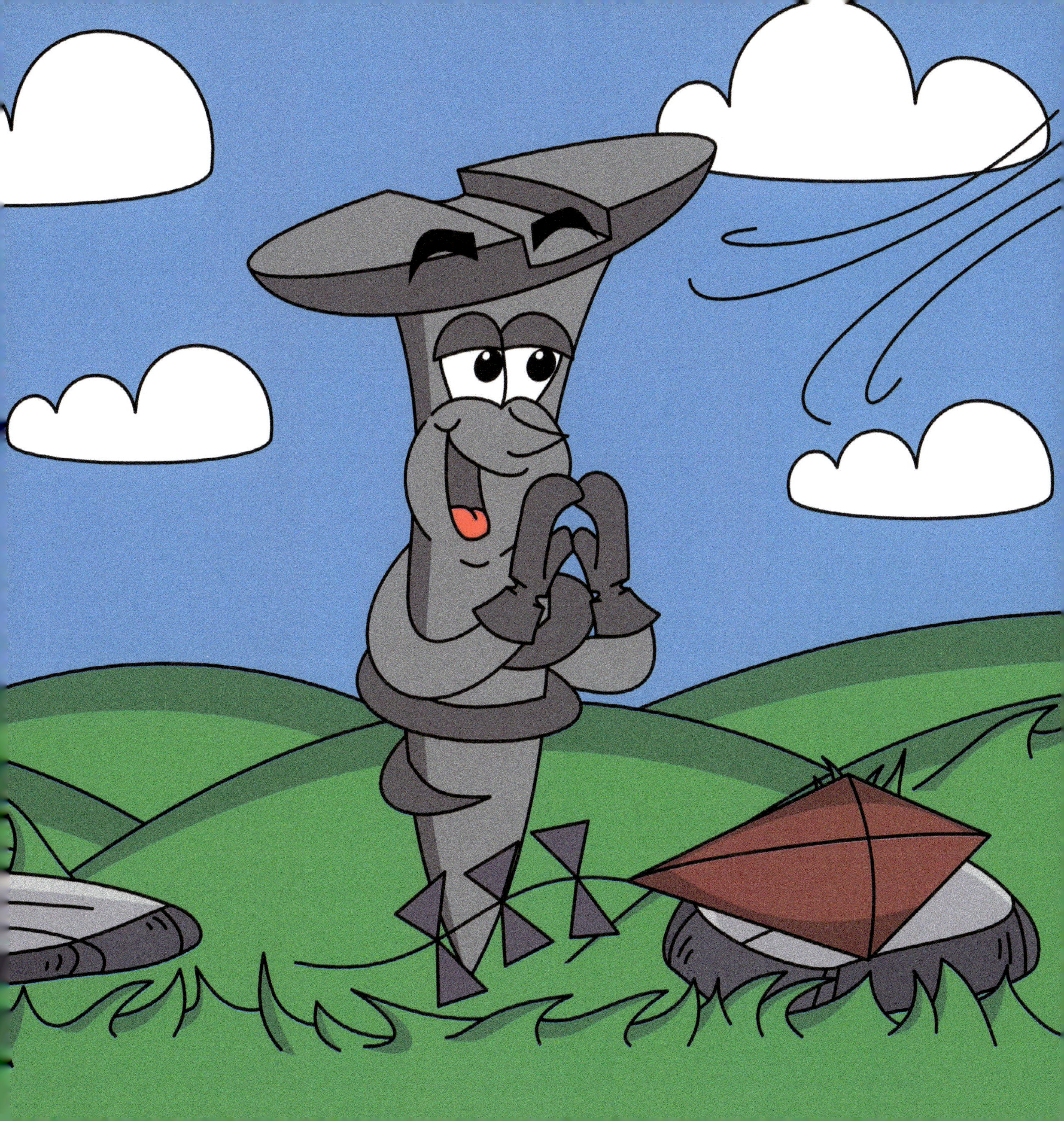

Screw licks a finger and
raises it to the sky.
One side grows cold as
the wind touches it.
Now Screw can feel where
the wind is coming from.

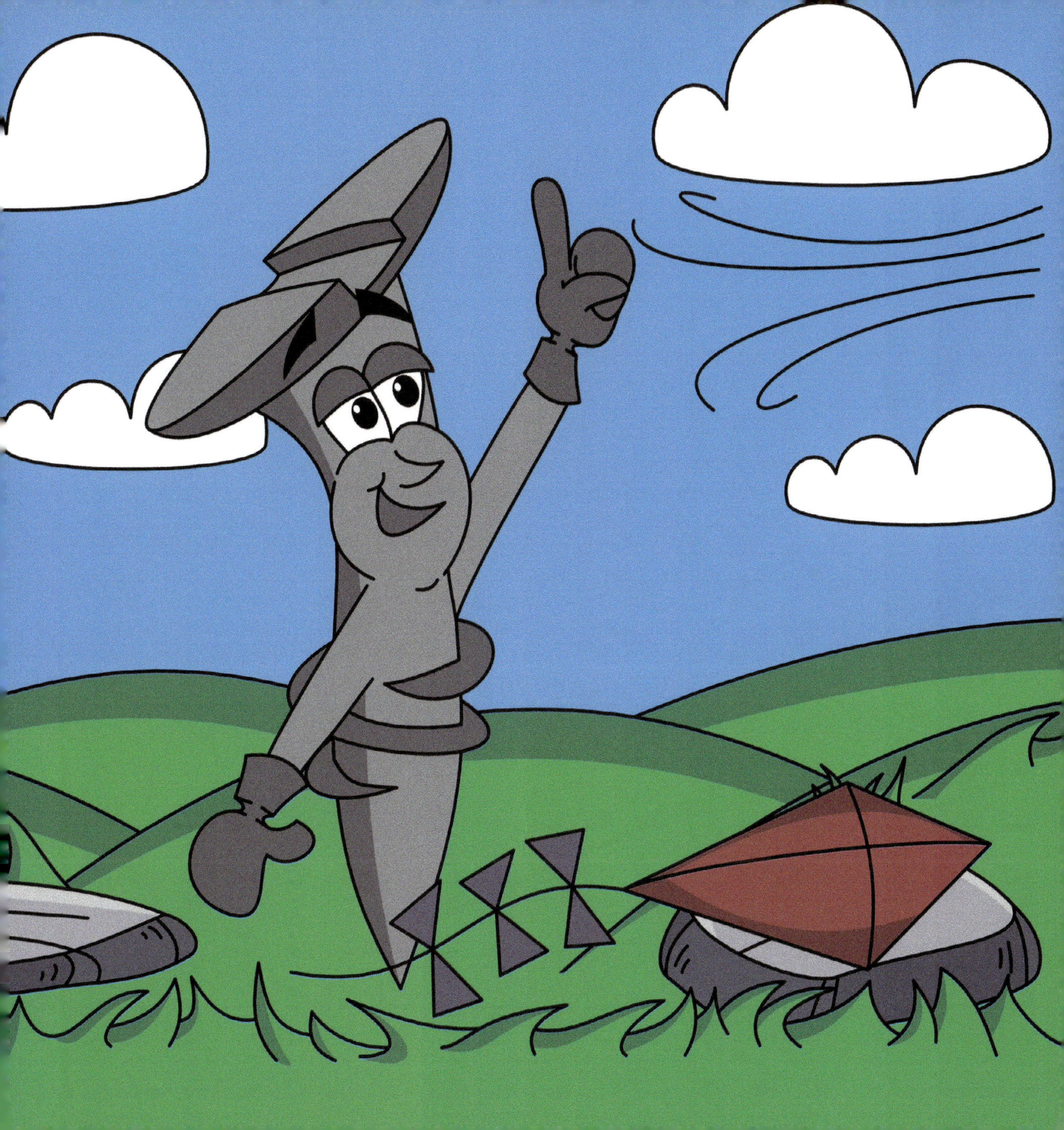

Screw runs towards the wind and the wind catches the kite.

It goes up and up and starts to fly.

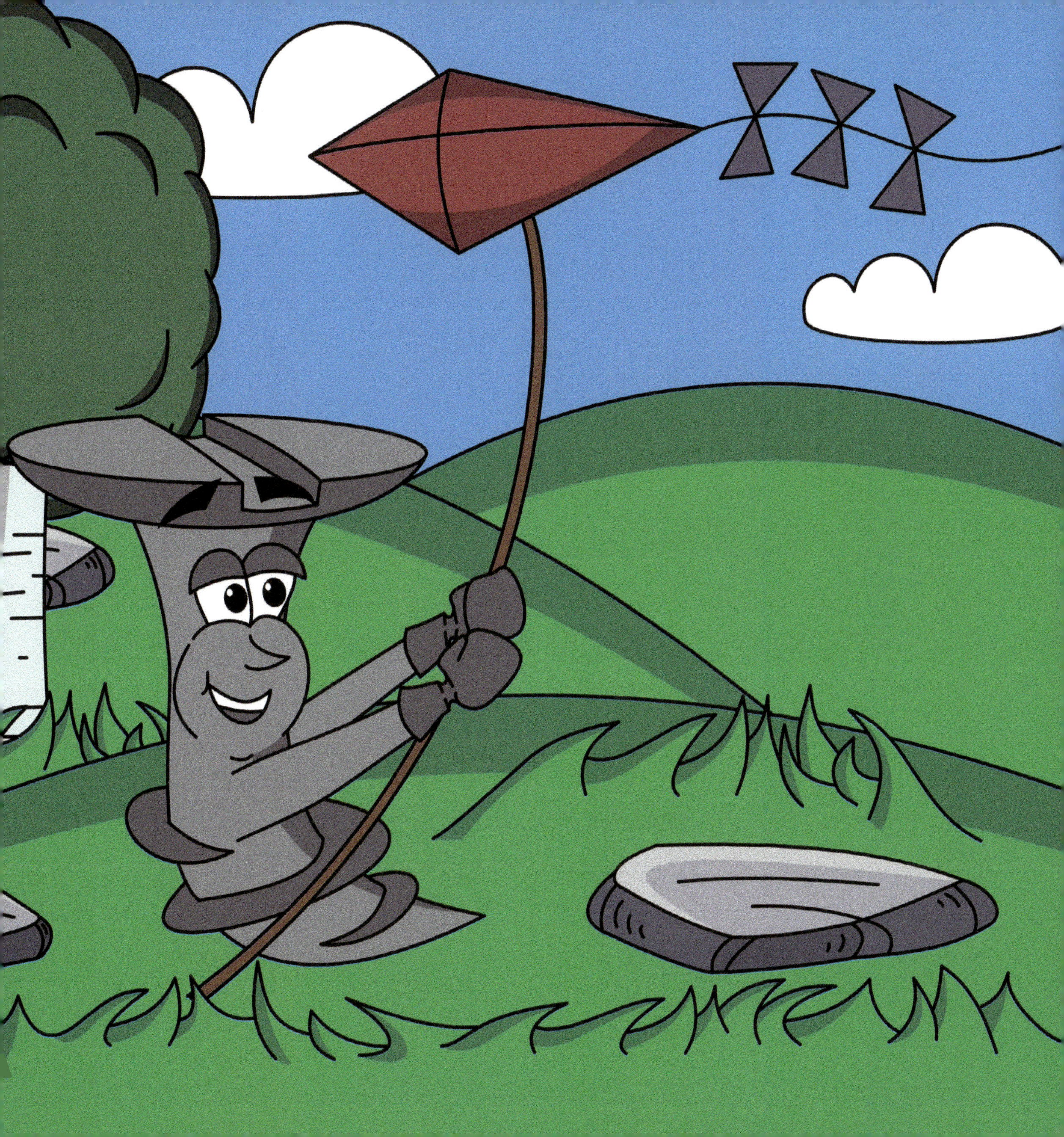

But then the wind starts
to blow more strongly.
It is really strong!
Screw is almost
blown away.

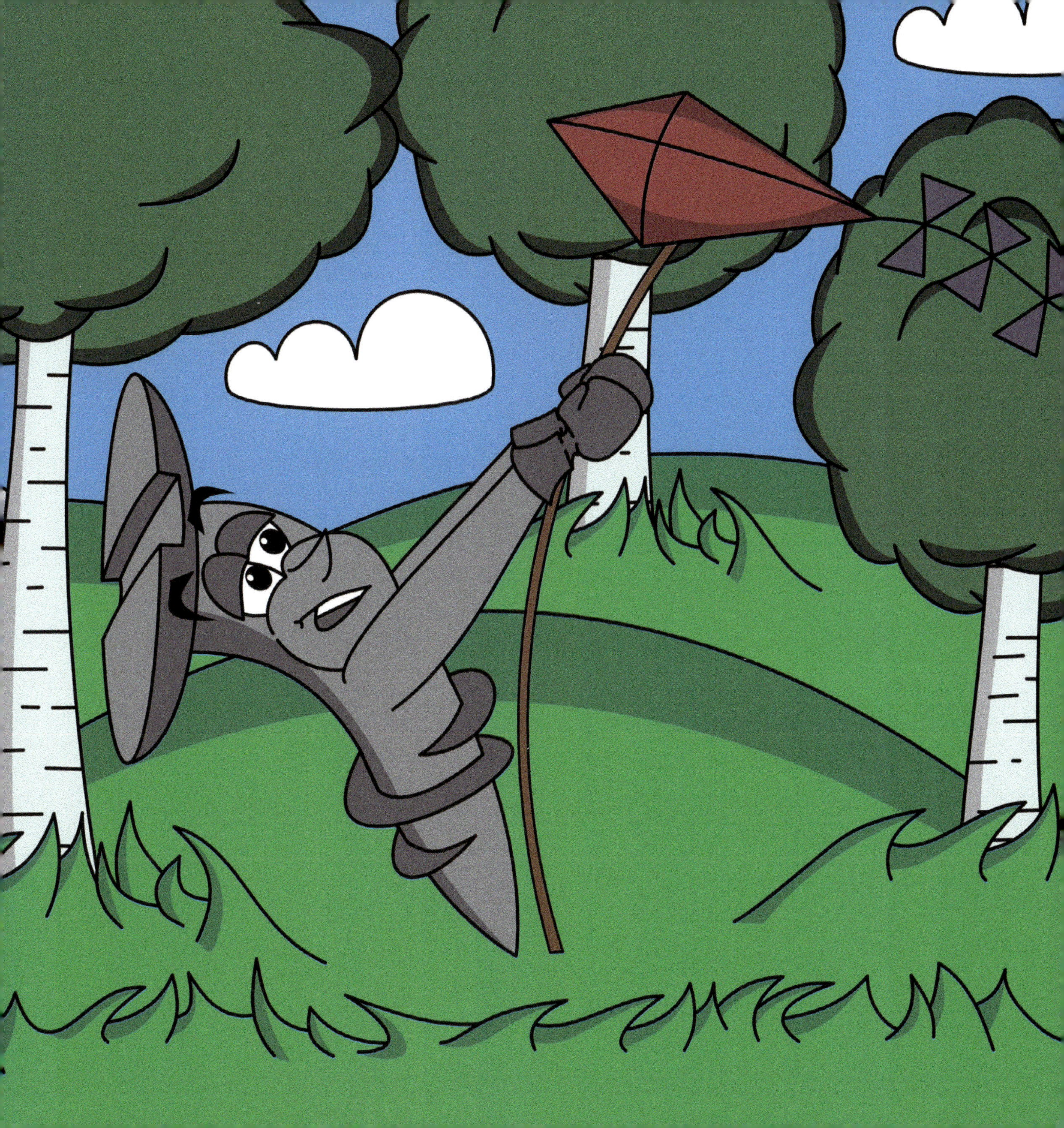

Screw clings to a tree while
the wind pulls the kite.
It's difficult to hold
on to it.

Oh dear! Screw is almost
losing it.

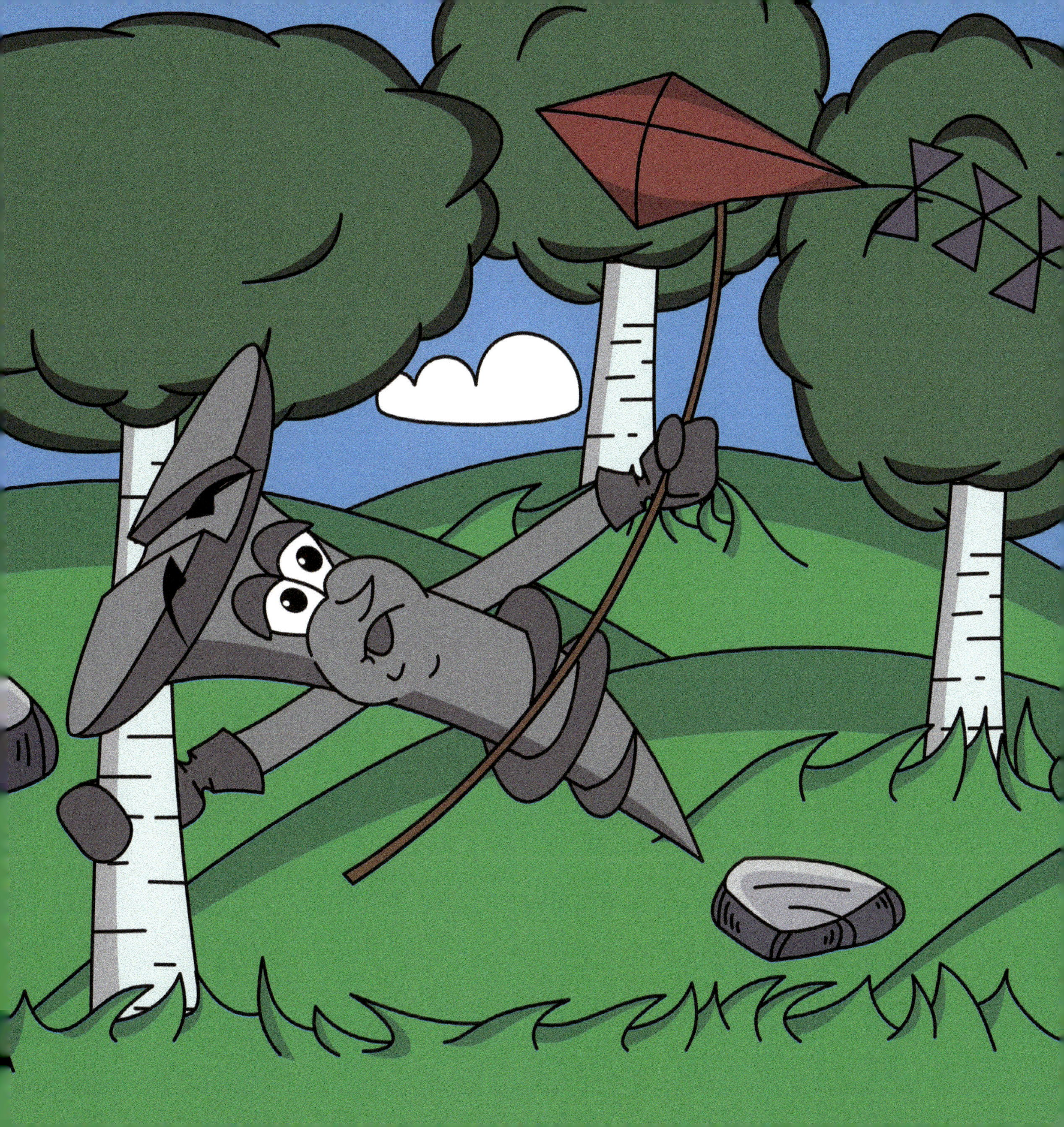

If Screw lets go, the kite will blow away and be lost! Screw must think of a way to solve the problem.

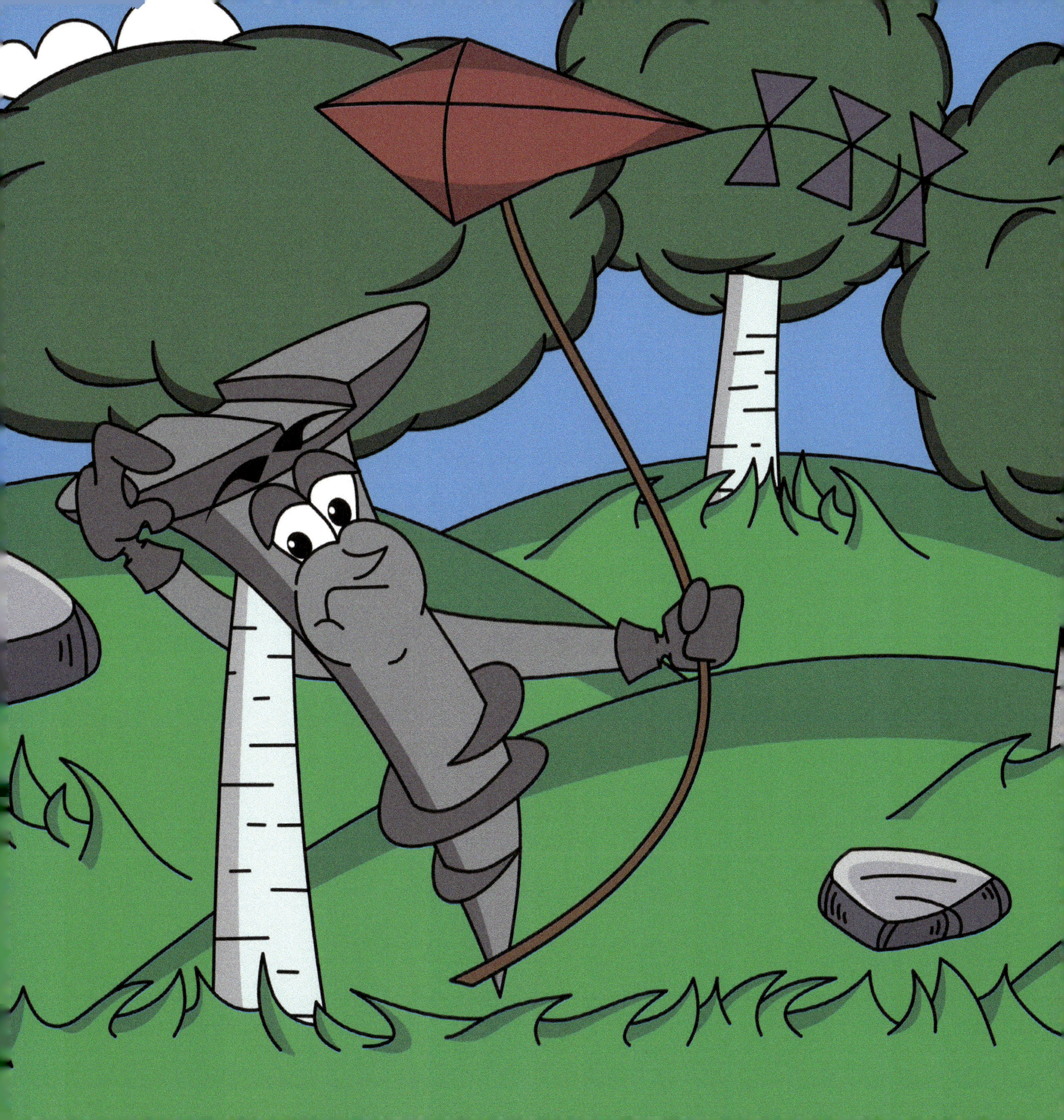

Then Screw has an idea.
'There is one way
I can stay firm.
I can use the ridges that run
around my stomach!
I can anchor myself to
the ground.'

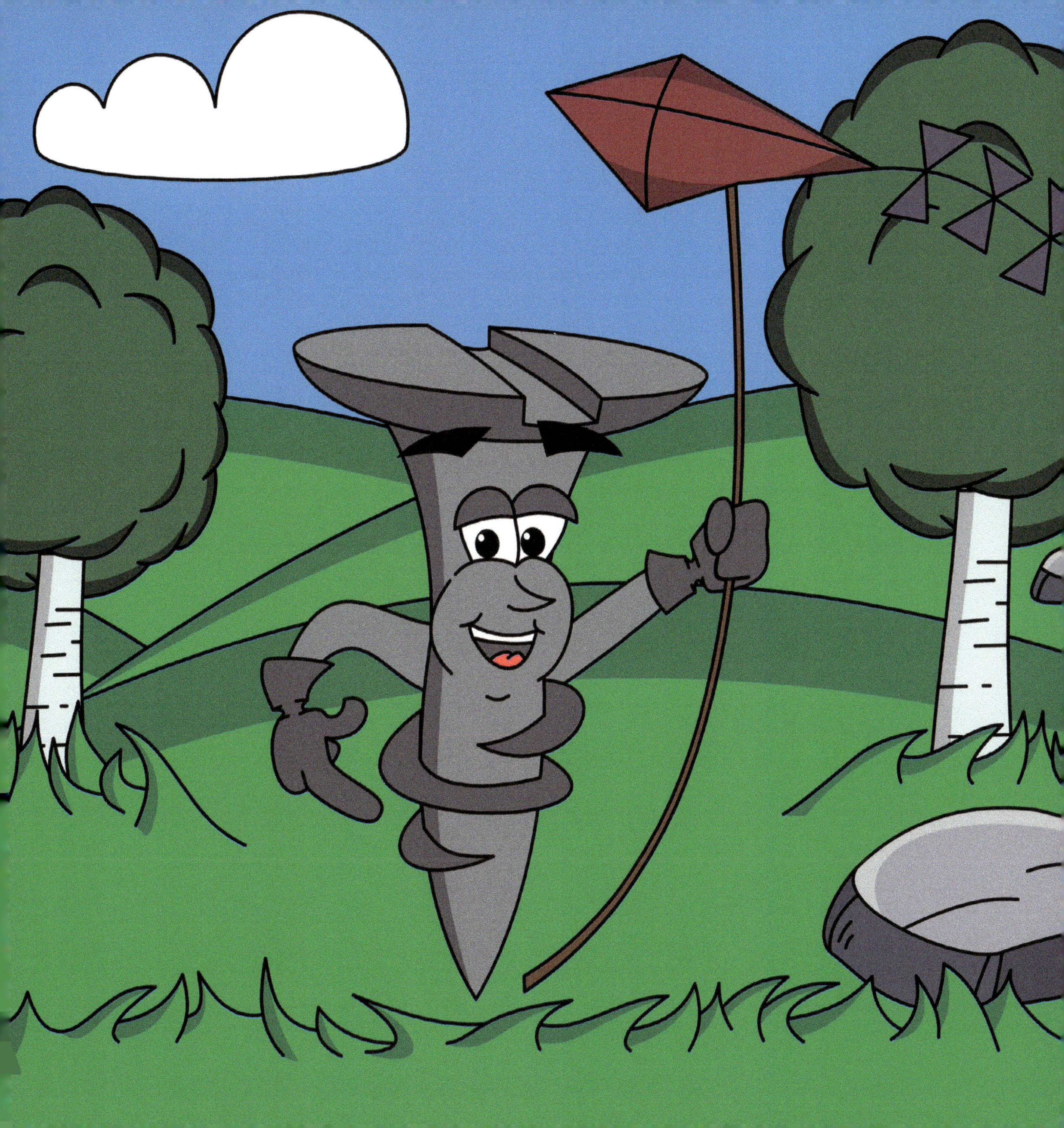

Screw turns around. Around and around. With each twist, Screw digs more deeply into the ground.

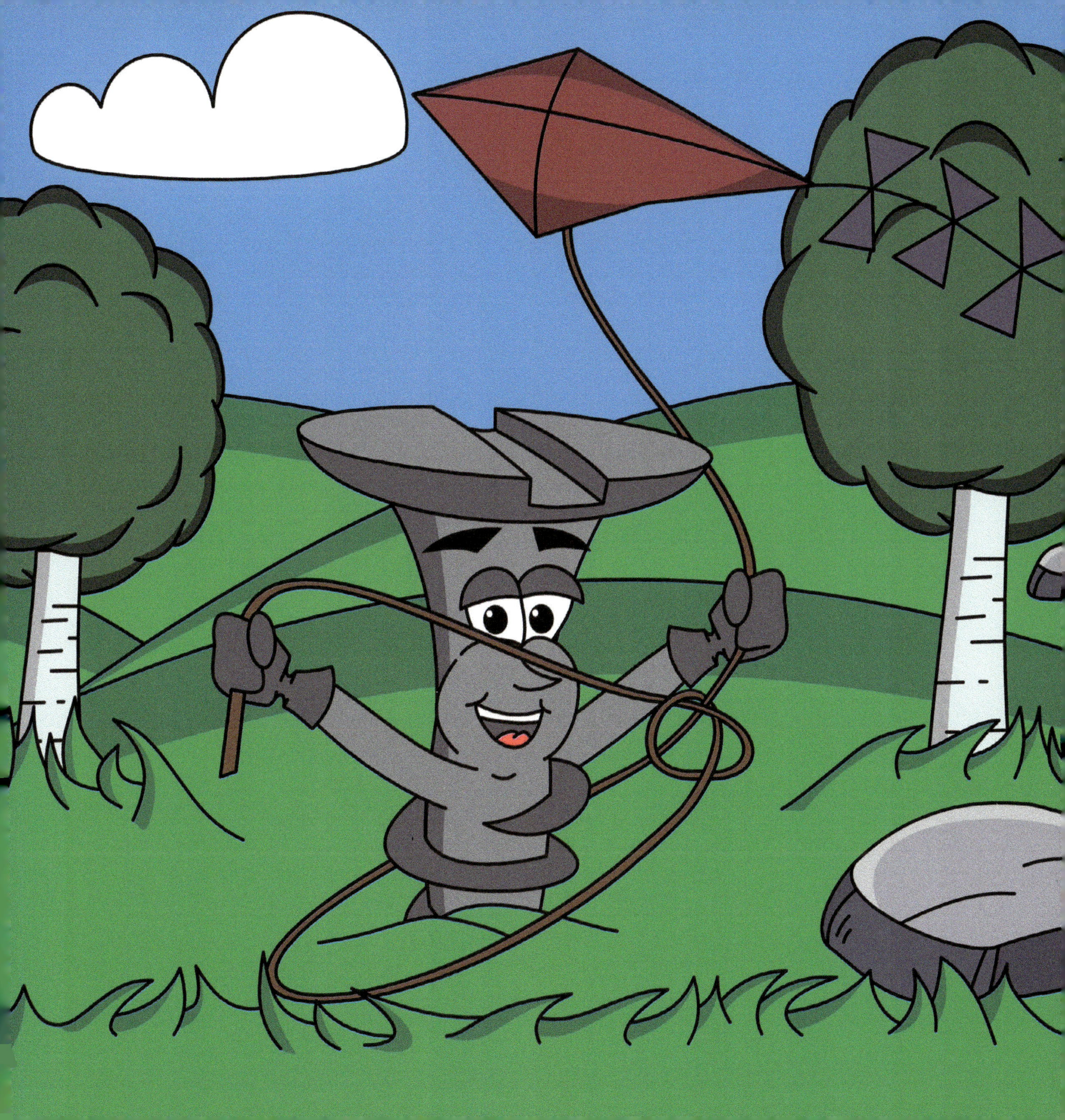

The string is tied firmly around Screw's stomach. Now there's no problem flying the kite in the strong wind.

It flies higher and higher.
What fun!

Soon the wind starts to die down and the kite lands gently on the grass.
It's time for Screw to twist the other way and pull out of the ground.

It's time to go home!

...Simple Machines...

Mattias Blomfeldt and Therese Karlsson are the authors of Simple Machines. They both work as preschool teachers and share an interest in making science and technology more popular and accessible to young children by highlighting them in stories of everyday life.

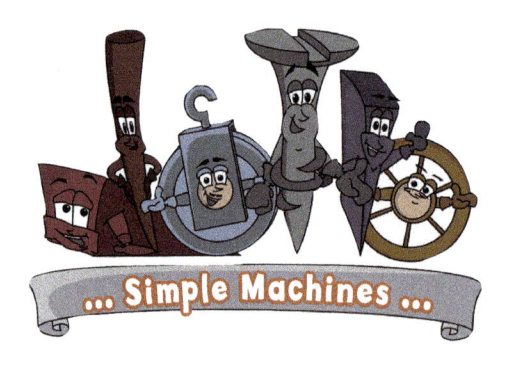

Mattias Blomfeldt
Text & Illustrations

Therese Karlsson
Text

TOMSING

Ellens backe 1, 694 30 Hallsberg
info@tomsing.se   www.tomsing.se

Copyright © The authors and TOMSING HB 2015
ISBN: 978-1-913189-08-2